Sanctuary
Meditative Heart
Mystical Love

LATONYA ENGON-ZIBI

Sanctuary of a Meditative Heart
Mystical Love

Copyright © 2019 by LaTonya Engon-Zibi

ISBN: 978-0-578-51743-8

DEDICATION

To Divine Mother, Father, Friend, Beloved, God
To those who have the Divine aflame in the
sanctuary of their hearts
To all who seek God everywhere all the time
And to those who feel pulled into contemplation by
these meditations and poems

Sanctuary of a Meditative Heart
Mystical Love

CONTENTS

ACKNOWLEDGMENTS

I give special thanks and appreciation to my parents,
Hezekiah and Gladys Foreman and to my sister, Umeka
Foreman for believing in this creation.
I express sincere gratitude to all of my readers who found
this creation and gave it a chance.
Thanks to my Beloved for the gifts that have been given for
me to be able to express my love to.

LOVE

Within my soul
Cryeth seven-fold
To reach Thee Heart of Mine

But Thee Heart is still
Yet gazes til
In search of Love's Divine

MOSH PIT

Throw me into the mosh pit of God
That I be held a prisoner thereof
Plummeting into God-silence
The voice of my Beloved

Breathless and stillness
Live and let death
Embraced by Mother
Thy Husband, Thy Mesh

SKY

Beautiful clouds of plush and white
As far as my eyes do see
Mother, Friend, Beloved, God
My sweet Divinity

HEAVENLY JOY

Behold hitherto I see
Saints and angel-cherubims
Clothed in the Light aphrodisiac
Dancing sweet beatific hymns

LOVE UNSPOKEN
Standing silently naked
Amidst the Winter's cold
Reminiscing a Summer lover
A Blue Jay sings her ode:

"Breasts adored once with pieces
Angelic greens and golds
Smiling her tentacle tresses
Capturing the Summer's soul

She whispered through her limbs
Soothing him cooling gestures
He replied so calm and tenderly warm
Giving kisses and blessing cares

Flattered by such breathless kisses
Blessed a many remnant fell
Revealing a tender light
His heart melts deep and tells

A love shining warm indeed
Within her God he kept
Glistening strong passions
Solemnly he peacefully wept

Time looked on a mute
Feeling such love a plight
Streaming counting tears
The dawning of Summer's night

Once the tide rides a shore
And the moon begins to set
Time will ring his seasonal alarm
Stealing Summer from whence he beget

Summer knew the secret
Yet he did not tell her
Instead he loved her until that day
And embraced her as it were

So, here she stands still-fully naked
Loved by the Winter's breeze
Until the secret comes alive
And Spring arrives to leave"

This is the song the Blue Jay sung
As he felt it in her heart
He too had a secret
He would soon have to part

However, loving her he continued to sing
Until time whispers him away
He would come back soon he knew
And sing another day

I AM

When the storm is raging be still
In the midst of chaos
Delusion is willed
When the senses are muted
And silence is drawn
The truth comes forth
And delusion is wronged
Then you will know
I had always been
Silently comforting your every whim
Because you remember Me
I Am

PREM (LOVE)

Your smile the essence of God
It speaks louder than words
The joy on your face
In that Light it favors

And when you do speak
My heart surely weeps
From the beauty of that Spirit
My soul doth seek

So, bliss I fall
Bliss I rise
While Heaven mirrors back at me
Through your eyes

Blessing me
Blessed be
The sanctuary of your heart
Your sweet nectared divinity

By how that love expresses itself
Oh!...I do feel
Invading my every atom
Silencing me tranquil

So, breathless I am
Yet restless all the same
From the beauty of your Spirit
And the Spirit of your name

SILENCE

He pierces my sigh
With His third eye
Mute am I to speak

Instead I feel
With Lover's seal
And express my Heart's unique

BEAUTIFUL BIRD

Look at the bird
High in the sky
Look at it soar
Look at it fly

Look at its duration
Light flight in blue tears
Look with admiration
How swift and how clear

Humming beautiful songs
Sweet praise and purity
Reflection of passion
Divine Simplicity...

Meekness of the bird
Slows down to a gentle rest
Last hymn of praise
Weak and once finessed

Grass blades cradle the beauty
Last breath-soul is love
Embraced by mourning tears
Dew drops of God's Love

HOME

I pray to that Brook
That runlet though my heart
With the sound of Love calling
From which Thou Art

Whispering opal-violet
Caressed by a stroke of gold
Leading me to the Star of David
Where my Father abodes

Singing waterfall bliss'
Which flood my soul
That glimmer with her kisses
And touches me bold

I wait for her gentle song
To carry me Home
On the shores of my devotion
AUM

FORGET ME NOT

Mother,
May Thy will be done
In whatever You entreaty
Simply draw me ever so close
And never forget me

But if Thou must forget me
Let it only be for a little while
Seek me and forsake me not
Your sweet and humbled child

DEATH

What is death…
But an earthly rest
When the body attests
And the soul is left

Then is there death
Since soul had been
Therefore is
And will for then?

SALVATION

It scratches out my eyes
Claws out my heart
Leaving me sockless
My chest ripped a part

Falling to my knees
Three holes in my flesh
Shadows of light piercing
Through my holy darkness

I feel for the emptiness
That echoes through my wounds
I pray out to the Angels
And the Saints to commune

Abba, El Shaddai!
My praise balled in my fist
Elohim, YHWH!
Grace feels my deepen pits

The wonder of this salvation
I do embrace and behold
My Beloved, Lord, Heavenly Maker
To relieve my soul!

Amen

RELIGIOUS

Lay ho' my soul surely weeps
Crying tears of supple kisses
Allah, Narankar, Hu, Brahman, Elohim
Rosary beads, mantra, the religious

AWAKENING

Silence is her voice calling
Abiding where time exceeds
The abyss of Her coming
The richness of Her bereave

SEEKING

I seek Thee in silence
I seek Thee in noise
I seek Thee in sadness
I seek Thee in joy

I seek Thee in the nights
I seek Thee in the days
I seek Thee in every corner
I seek Thee in every way

Wilt Thou not come?

Oh God! Wilt Thou not come?
I seek Thee with no rest
I seek Thee with my life
And I will seek Thee til my death!

WAITING

Visit me as a surprise
Linger so that I may joy
Whisper to me like the coming waves
Beckon me out of coy

Come as a nightly thief
Awaken me from slumber
Excite to me Your mystery
Leave me unencumbered

I imagine with calm eagerness
I am the damsel in distress
I am the mistress elite
I am the secret Cindereless

I am also the lover You knew
And the lover You've always known
I am waiting for You my Beloved
To arrest my soul alone

THE GAME

Keep God's grace upon your face
Praise Her Holy name
Know life has challenges - walk through the valley
Life is a spiritual game

SURRENDER

Hold on to the Holy
The Spirit that guides you
If you know that He truly exists
Don't doubt the Love and just believe
Thinking that you are taking a risk

LOVE IN THE NIGHT

Oh beautiful Night!
What cometh of You
But darkness with a hint of bright
And varying shades of hue

Your quiet sings me asleep
Your calm is a silent chime
Your touch reveals my shallows
The awakening of Your soul and mine

Oh, I love You my Night!
And shining armor my dear
The kiss of Your black pearls
Revealing my shadow sheer

I surrender all
My melatonin guise
To the sway of Your night fall
My temperantal eyes

TO WHAT AVAIL

My life is destined to nothing
My death futilely the same
My works, prayers, hopes and dreams
Mean nothing yet mean everything

FUSION

Come back to take me Aum
The sound of millions of buzzing bees awaken me
The motor of my soul in Yours

Your Light reaching for me
Like the moon drawing closer to the earth
The sun setting upon me
Our union of love

MOTHER

I love you deeper than you know-
Wasting away in a lover's trance
Gone are the days of thinking
My catatonic stance

I love you deeper than you know-
What am I to do?
I love you so much
I wish you were not you

I wish you were not born
It causes so much pain
I wish I never knew you
My pierced heart love-stained

Because you are so lovely
Beauty that eternity can not transcend
The depth of such love
No alpha or omega fends

And yet it is not you
From where I derive such pain
It is the One who created you
Where I place this blame

I understand...
It is Divine Mother that created you
Placing Her essence in my being
To love that which is you

Good God I am in Love!
I have gone graciously insane
Intoxicated by Divine Mother
Thy eternal Love aflame

I love you deeper than you know

FEELING

I cry to the thought of You loving me
Can this love I feel be You?
I, crying for You
While You cry for me too?

THE BUMBLE BEE

There was something in my pocket
I rubbed and rubbed it gay
It felt like a small bundle of paper
But oh to my dismay!

I pulled it out of my pocket
Guess what I saw?
A yellow stoned bumble bee
Sluggish from rubbing it raw

It walked slowly on the ground
Drunken to a stop
Amazed it didn't sting me
I blessed her for having not

RESPONSE TO MY PRAYERS
The darkness receives my prayers
While the moon slumbers
Hiding in the veil
Lurks the silence of thunder
Echoing the lightning rods of my urgent cares

GOD-FILLED

Oh God!..how much I love You!
I think of You everyday
I think of You in every way
Then I don't think...
I don't think at all
I am like a wall
Silent and unassuming
Present and exhuming
Here and not
Full and tot
Of You

REMEMBER

Remember to be nice
Remember to be kind
Remember to be lovely
As a representative of the Divine

BLISS

Mother, as I go within the meditation of my heart
I am pulled into the Black hole of Yours
In galactic submission
Parachuting in Cosmic bliss
Held and sustained
In the womb of amniotic ecstasy

ACTION

Thank You for the Cosmic picture show
Shadow forms created in suspended rapture
Moving in a dance of pulsating Light
Your Thought-filled Energy and Love

TURN DOWN THE LIGHT

I saw You nearing
Yet scurried to sleep
To avoid Your coming
To merge us to meet

Your bright Light hovering
Drawing closer to mine
My light reserved
To prevent our Love entwine

You tried for several nights
My fear declined this desire
Instead I denied Your Bright
Turned down to go Higher

I became regretful and frustrated
When You eventually gave up
Because I had craved Your Love
But didn't feel worthy enough

So, I cleanse my body
I cleanse my mind
I covet spirit
To be ready next time

And for this reason
I fervently wait
For You to come again
And to consummate

Our Love, our Joy, our Bliss!

MASTER

Breathe in, breathe out
Pause...death
Breath in...resurrect
Master of myself

GIVE

I have been hurt...
By my sister, my brother
I give these tears and pain
To You, Divine Mother

YOU

Father, I want of nothing
But to see You in everything
To desire You only
My sweet and melodic King

MARK

The mark of the green
That encompasses my face
How beautiful and ugly
I am
A reminder of my birth
That reveals Thy grace
The truth and distort
I flam

QUIET ROOM

I sit in silence
While listening to the rain
Fall like the soft crackles of a kindling fire
Against the window pane

Tap dancing raindrops
Sliding down the glass
Revealing grey-stained overtones
In the throws of a quiet mass

In my room

WILL OF NATURE

The birds are the birds
Heavenly do they sing
Beauty to my soul
Wisdom in their serenading

And

The spider how meticulous the spider
Such mystery webs from them
Beauty to my soul
Wisdom in their limbs

And

The rock is the rock
Hard, peaceful and still
Beauty to my soul
Wisdom in its will?

And

The moon is the moon
How round is the moon
Beauty to my soul
Wisdom in its Fortune

And

The rain is the rain
How dainty does it dance
Beauty to my soul
Wisdom in its prance

And

The lover is the lover
Oh! the desire of the lover
Beauty to my soul
Wisdom in her ferver

And

My Mother is the Divine Mother
The Light within all these
Beauty of my soul
Wisdom in Her Being

GOD

Infinite beyond immortal
Sweeter than ecstasy I am sweet
The taste of Love loving
Caressing liberal's aesthete

LIGHT

Light Am I
The Light...
Transparent and lucid
Beyond subtle bright

REVEAL

The burning of my flesh
Illuminating my soul
Melting away desires
Stifled passions cajoled

GOD'S COMFORT

In the midst of that thing told of:
When troubles appear a drinking hole
And days seem less visible
And life seems cold

And your tears may fail
Or fail to fall
As anger rages a mighty blow
And you struggle to squall

Or the skies color gray
That cry your bane
While the wind blows you awkward
As you wither and wane

The flowers withdrawing their fragrances
And the grasses die flat
Trees violently thrashing bigotries
Mimicking your slack

And the birds sing for you not
And the mountain falls down
Men seem violent
Scolding your grounds

When your hand reaches for love
And grapples with nothing plain
And life seems miserable
Leaving you un-toughed and maimed

Know God's comfort

BELOVED

Seek the Beloved
Know that He is Seeking
And has sought

Cry for the Beloved
Know that He is the tears
And is crying

Feel the Beloved
Know that She is the feeling
And has felt

Sing for the Beloved
Know that She is the song
And is singing

Love the Beloved
Know that She is Love
And the Lover

MY LOVE

My soul felt...
It wanted to Know
Yet it was content to the liking
But somehow a spark was lit by the soul's uniting

The spark flew out and away
Like a shooting star disappearing in the sky

Where did it go?

SAINTS AND DEVOTION
Jesus, Mohammed, St. John of the Cross,
Gandhi, Mother Teresa
Dalai Lama, Sri Muktananda
St. Teresa of Avila
Parmahansa Yogananda, Francis of Assissi,
Amachi, Sri Ramakrishna, Thomas Merton of
Gethsemani,
St. Thomas, St. Lynn, Moses, Abraham,
Krishnamurti, the Virgin Mary, Khalil Gibran
Saints of all religions and traditions
Blessed Be Thy names
Saints and Masters of Thy God
I gratefully and lovingly proclaim

LIFE

To Life that is all yet naught
My soul seize Your kiss
And halycon days of heart
Of sweet immortal bliss

To You I note this honor
Euphonious is Your name
Blithe is Your resistance
And the mystery of Your fame

Your beginning seems abyss
The ending dare not tell
Your right is sometimes pending risks
The wrong believed to hell

Your worth is damned about
Though praised all the same
Your truth is faithfullly sought
Though lies prove Your gain

Honoring You a valor
The sweetest symphony
My heart is-in loving
Your essential entire Being

DIVINE CHEMISTRY

I slip on the flame
The embers cloaking me
The smoke, my perfume
The alchemy, my desire
Transformed into surrender
Simmered down to peace
And returned to innocence

OPEN HEART
Saint!
Light the candle!

Light this place up!
Light up this darkness
Shine the Light on every wall
Shine the Light on every vessel
Take it down each chamber
And when the Light begins to fickle
Blow it out and let the fumes run free
Watch as worry, anger and doubt dissipate
While compassion, love and peace linger

Then affirm a kind word or two
Speak loud!
Let your words echo through these chambers
Imprinting this place with the Love of God
Resonating and binding the truth
To renew devotion of this heart

DESIRE

Speak to me in symphony
Shamanize my bliss
Bring me back to reality
And leave me with Your kiss

ANANDA OF MASTER

I look at you with discipline
Inspired by your gaze
Eyes focused outward yet deep within
The longing state I cave
To be the longing that you possess
The perfect merger of Earth and Spirit
Outside of and inside of you
As I desire to also draw near it

FREEDOM

I am in love with surrender
The promises that it brings
The oath that it holds
The trust that it clings

THE ROSE IN THE VASE

She slay limp in the water
Hung over the edge
Held by simple glass

Relieved by the days of her life
Drunken with death lingering
To the secrets of her life to pass

That God instilled into her

ARMAGEDDON

Guide my mind to what is good
When evil comes...
Tell the Angels to whisper in my ear
While devils play with my heart
In my house of contemplation
Keep the gate locked from thieves
When despair hits my pillow
Bring truth to my dreams
In my solitude
Be my watchdog from the growling air
When evil comes...
I will shake the devil's hand
And smile at her defense

AVE SOUL

Ode to the soul, the grace of God with Thee
Praise you little one
Blessed is the Love of Thy Lord
The Love of the soul
Meditate dear soul
To the coming of the Lord
AUM

LONE STAR

Lonely is and lonely does
My sweet valentine
Cry my baby
Hush sweet darling
Little star of mine

BLUE TO GOLDEN

The boat lies still in the water
The Light of God shown in it
The color of Blue daffodils
As the ocean washes against it

The sun Golden revealing a smile
The empty Blue boat with a past
Cleansed by the sea and sun
The forgotten wiped aghast

Let me tell you the story
The tale accompanying this Blue boat
Where wishes, hopes and dreams were tried
To support men to growth:

Three natives, wise and strong
Painted the sky with the whispers of their souls
Many colors painted the sky
But only Blue remained foretold

Blue permeated on all that it touched
The birds, the trees, and waters
The natives and strangers too indeed
All inhaled the Blue soul-filled modder

Only wonting souls were transformed
Love soothed their receptive hearts
But the tethered remained moderately Grey
Unable to ingest the Blue impart

Envious of the Blue
The tethered convinced the natives to Grey
Sharing lies of the wisemen's whispers
To keep the town affray

Deprived of the Blue blessing
The town had become deficit
The wisemen whispered Blue into the sky again
To keep the hearts of men arrested

But the town had become mulchy Black
The natives lie prey to the mortal belief
Drowning in the color of sorrow
The wisemen began to grieve

The wisemen whispered frozen
The coldness of natives Black
They called out to God
For guidance to take the town back

Blue winds filled the dual colored air
Where the wisemen firmly stood
God with a mighty blow
Kept en-light the wisemen's good

Drunken, the men fell
Their souls inhabiting a nearby tree
The tree in submission fell down
Sacrificing life for these wise three

Spirits ascended and descended marinating the tree
Into a Blue boat intoxicated-vessel
Floating, the men seized the Love-maiden boat
To escape the somber Black level

The ocean rising high as the mountains
The Blue boat in distress
As God blew among the sea
To move the boat afresh

Blue was the color of the sea
As God guided the men to shore Golden
The tier of their souls' destiny
To salvage the wise their foreboden

Ah! the wisemen sighed
As they rose upon the Gold
With a million suns in wait
To welcome the wise natives expansive souls

Ah! God then sighed
With the breath of many Lights
That fell upon the men
And enlightened their Blue to pure Light

To God be the Glory
To Light the ways of men
Thou they may fall to Black
The Light is always there again and again

For those who seek to share the Blue
And to reach for the Gold to Bright
Blessed be your efforts
To share this Love of Light

ACCEPTANCE

Accept the yes and the no
Accept the maybe so
Accept the uncertainty
Accept the will to go...

TRUST I

No matter the matter
I trust Thee still
I am loyal to Thee
With my free will

TRUST II

I may fall and wonder
Confused and with distaste
But I am willing and trustful
To redirect each mistake

TRUST III

To trust seems hard
When things fall sway
Yet to trust is the crust
To overcome dismay

TRUST IV

To go with or against the self is a choice
Neither is right nor wrong
Yet one may fair...the other may not
To create the path short or long

WITH ME

I sit down and You hold me up
I lay down and You mold my body

I stand tall and Your gravity holds me upright
I may kneel and You keep me centered

I close my eyes and You are still there
Eyes open You are everywhere

I blink and I am on both sides with You
I stare and You put me in a trance

I touch my legs and we walk together
I noted Your four legs walking across my floor

I've seen You web in the corner of my room with eight
More than eight when Your body is long

I touch my heart and feel You
When I breathe You fill me

I feel You land on my skin
I felt Your breath as the wind

I utter Your name and I am inspired
I think Your name and You are a mystery

Felipe is Your name as well as Coreana
You are the names of all names

You are the one that holds me
You see me

You walk with me
You feel me
And You know who I am

GREAT

I sit quiet in my room
Looking around at everything
The sofa, the paintings on the wall
The hat that hangs from my closet door
And I embrace the silence to ponder
How Great Thou Art

LONGING I

I can't stop thinking of You
Do You think of me the same?
I whisper for You softly
Do You also whisper my name?

LONGING II

I desire for what is quite Unknown
Do You desire what You know?
I look for You in a daze
To find You in my soul!

BOUQUET

Take this flower
Each petal, I count my love for You
The stem, I hold You in my heart

Look inside and see the pattern of my soul
Over there from where I chose it
A bed full of flowers

Full...

TRANSCEND

My mind into Heaven
My feet standing upon the earth

The angels see
Spirits are moved
Humans are at a standstill

God is my witness

LOVE UNTAMED

A strong wave of love
Broke the dam of my heart
Flooded everything it touched

I tried to restrain it
But the force was too strong
It fused to everything it clutched

WITHIN

Fluid lies filter earth-filled eyes
Lust of the world to feed
Reverse the flow and come alive
To meet the Spirit's need

EMOTIONS I

God, control this tongue
Tame it right
Prevent me from firing
An angry spite

EMOTIONS II

God, hold this hand
Bend it back
Keep it from forwarding
An unloving slap

EMOTIONS III

God, soften these eyes
Calm them soft
Preserve my sighting
An untruthful accost

GUIDANCE

Lord guide my ways
To Love beyond any gifts given
To have a peace of mind
And a flourishing soul

READY

Eyes wide open
Mouth closed shut
Arms stretched out
Heart opened up

FULFILLING LOVE

Your Love
Fills me with bliss
Intoxicating me insensible
Your infinite kiss

GODDESS

She is beautiful
As of rite
With coarse mane hair
And diamond shaped eyes
That twinkle pure and clear
To the heart of Light
A gaze of grace
Which comforts the night

When her soul speaks
As flowing flowers and melodic birds
The glistening of Heaven reveals
Blessings by the serenity of her words
She is an Angel
A presence that goes without voice
An awe unspoken
Angelically coy

When she walks
The ground smiles at her feet
As her arms sway lightly
Her legs strong and sweet
She is felt when she arrives
And felt when she leaves
Her presence lingers
Likened to the wind wafting the leaves

She is kind and compassionate
Joyous and fun
An inspiration who oaths to good
Living in abundance

A healer, a transformer
Self-loving is she
The sacred, awakened,
Enlightened and free

Her smile perfectly warm
With a heart seemingly foretold
With the eye of a sparrow
And the essence of a rose

She is beautiful...

SACRED
Holy, blessed
Consecrated, promoted
Spiritual, religious
Ecclesiastic, devoted

STILLING SLOWLY

Silence draws near
I must prepare to end
To still these inspired thoughts

Yet one more thought lingers
Please read below
The Sanctuary of a Meditative Heart

SANCTUARY OF A MEDITATIVE HEART

I pray during the night
To the stillness of my heart
Where demons lie in waiting
And angels opt to thwart

To preserve my soul's devotion
Amidst the brooch of heaven and hell
I affirm my mandate to sparse
To victory of heaven's quell

In the haven of my heart
Where this battle is silenced still
The devils whims are excused
While the angels whims are fulfilled

Out of this comes good
Climbing the rung of my tempted path
To the tempest of my Love
Where God and I amass

In the sanctuary of my meditative heart
My soul is preserved
In the bosom of my Beloved
My Love, my Joy, my Reserve

ABOUT THE AUTHOR

LATONYA ENGON-ZIBI, a native of Tennessee, grew up with an inquisitive mind about nature, religion and God. She is a current graduate student studying theology at Boston University. She is a holistic practitioner, serving as both a psychotherapist and metaphysician in private practice in Cambridge, Massachusetts.

Printed in Dunstable, United Kingdom